# *The* WISDOM *of*
# OMAR KHAYYAM

# *The* WISDOM OF

# OMAR KHAYYAM

A SELECTION OF QUATRAINS
TRANSLATED FROM THE PERSIAN

BY

## EBEN FRANCIS THOMPSON

PHILOSOPHICAL LIBRARY, INC.

New York

*Distributed to the Trade by*
BOOK SALES, INC.
352 Park Avenue South
New York 10, N.Y.

Manufactured in the United States of America

# INTRODUCTION

Omar Khayyam was born in the first half of the eleventh century A. D. at Nishapur, in the province of Khorasan, Persia, and died in 1123 A. D.

Although his most famous work is the *Rubaiyat,* of which the present book is a distillation, he wrote several other poetical works, dealing primarily with scientific subjects in a philosophical vein.

Much of Khayyam's philosophy was of a nature to challenge the hostility of the orthodox Mussulman, and his manuscripts were doubtless the object of the destructive zeal of the pious. It is small wonder, then, that the reputation of Khayyam the poet was obscured by that of Khayyam the astronomer and mathematician, and that the seeds of his poetry and philosophy should have lain dormant in the dust of eight centuries.

*The Wisdom of Omar Khayyam* consists of a selection of 365 of the most sagacious and comely quatrains from the *Rubaiyat.* The Rubaiyat quatrain, or Ruba'i, is a four line stanza that has from ten to thirteen syllables in a line and rhymes in the first, second and fourth lines, and occasionally in all four. Each Ruba'i constitutes a complete and distinct poem in itself, and in this form is a purely Persian invention.

Any attempt to epitomize the character of Omar Khayyam as it is reflected in his writings would be a difficult task, so varied and contradictory are the quatrains. Written at different periods covering a long life, they often express a transient mood. Nevertheless, two hallmarks of character run throughout his work—his mysticism and a sense of good fellowship, both informed by a strong human sympathy and audacity in dealing with theological dogma and metaphysical mystery.

# Quatrains

### 1

Let not your soul in Sorrow's clasp be prest,
Nor let your days be filled with vain unrest;
    The book, the loved one's lips and marge
        of mead
Forsake not ere Earth fold you in her breast.

### 2

I'll counsel give, if you will list to me,
Don not the garment of Hypocrisy,
    This life is but a breath, the next all time,
For that one breath sell not Eternity.

### 3

Drink wine! for when to dust your body turns,
Your clay becomes thereafter cups and urns,
    Of Hell or Heaven reck not, for pray why should
A wise man be deceived in such concerns?

### 4

No night my cry doth not reach Gemini,
That my tears' current flows not to the sea;
    "After to-morrow" say'st "I'll drink with thee?"
Life e'en that morrow may not reach for me!

### 5

This vase like me a hapless lover pined
In snares of beauty's tresses once confined;
    This handle on its neck you see was once
An arm oft round the loved one's neck entwined.

## 6

On that Day when the good rewards receive,
May I, a suppliant sot, a share derive!
  Let the Fates count me with the good, if good,
Or with the bad, if bad, may They forgive!

## 7

So go about that men salute thee ne'er;
With folk live that from comment they forbear;
  So enter mosques that they ne'er summon thee
In front, nor thee appoint to lead in prayer!

## 8

Whose heart so ever love lights, whether he
The mosque attend or church frequenter be,
  Hath his name written in the book of Love
From thought of Paradise or Hell set free.

## 9

The idol spoke thus to the devotee,
"Dost thou know how thou cam'st to worship me?"
    "Through me His beauty hath He caused to
      shine,
Who, oh my witness, vision gives to thee."

## 10

Where in yon palace Bahram wine-cup prest,
The roe bears young, the lion oft takes rest,
    King Bahram who in noose oft caught the *Gur*,
See how the *Gur* hath Bahram caught at last!

## 11

Since long in earth you'll sleep, the goblet drain,
For far from friend, mate, consort, you'll remain.
    Take care this secret you do not reveal,
"No withered tulip ever blooms again."

O, thou! whose cheeks surpass the eglantine!
Whose lovely face outvies the maids of Chin!
    Thy one glance giv'n my fond king yestere'en
Moved knight and bishop, castle, pawns and queen!

Life's caravan moves on in mystery,
Seize then the joyous moments as they fly.
    Why fret, boy, o'er the morrow of thy friends?
Bring forth the cup, for night is hast'ning by!

To him who o'er his sins doth easy seem,
Let pious people make this point their theme;
    "To say 'God's wisdom is the cause of sin,'
To men of sense seems ignorance extreme."

## 15

Zealots know not as we Thy clemency;
The stranger as the friend cannot know Thee;
    Thou say'st, "If thou sin I'll cast thee to Hell."
Tell that to him who knows not Thee as we.

## 16

Though creeds some two and seventy there be,
The first of creeds I hold is love of Thee;
    What of obedience, Islam, unfaith, sin?
Thou'rt all my aim, the rest be far from me!

## 17

Last night, wine flown, the tavern passing, I
A graybeard, drunk and jar on back, did spy,
    I said, "Old man, 'fore God, have you no shame?"
"From God comes mercy, drink!" was his reply.

## 18

The Sun flings morning's noose o'er dome and tower,
Day's king Khosrau, wine in the bowl doth pour;
    Drink! For the rising Herald of the Morn
Greeting the days proclaims the dawning hour.

## 19

Arise and come, for my heart's solace, pray
This state of doubt with thy charm take away,
    And bring a jug of wine that we may drink
Ere potters fashion wine-jars from our clay!

## 20

Destiny's curtain none can penetrate,
Nor learn the hidden mysteries of Fate,
    Seventy-two years I've pondered day and night,
Nor solve aught—long the tale were to relate!

I drink my wine, for men like me of sense
In God's sight 't is of little consequence;
 He knew it at the first, if I drink not
Sheer ignorance would be God's prescience!

O, Kh'aja! grant us one wish, only one.
Be still! with our affairs with God have done!
 We walk aright, 't is you who see awry,
Go you and cure your sight, leave us alone!

Heaven whispered to my spirit secretly,
"The fixed decrees of Fate learn thou from me,
 If I in my own turnings had a hand,
Myself from dizziness I 'd have set free!"

### 24

A cup! for He who did this clay combine,
Of love and drink on our heads wrote the line;
  With beauties and with wine the world is filled,
But only promised are Heaven's maids and wine!

### 25

Wash me with grape juice when life ebbs away,
And "parting words" with wine and wine-cup say;
  If me ye 'd find on Resurrection Morn,
In dust of tavern thresholds seek my clay.

### 26

Since no one can the morrow guarantee,
To-day this woeful heart make glad in thee;
  Drink wine in moonlight, O Moon, for the moon
Will shine full often nor find thee nor me.

## 27

Love, though a curse, is made so by God's sway,
Then why should God His blight upon us lay?
    Since Good and Bad are creatures of His will
Why for His slaves hath He a Reck'ning Day?

## 28

Cupbearer, bowl and wine by marge of dell
Are Heaven enough for me and thee as well;
    Hear not from any talk of Hell or Heaven,
For whoe'er came from Heaven or went to Hell?

## 29

Who brings thee to me rapt at close of day,
Who leads thee from the harem on thy way?
    To him who in thine absence burns as fire,
When leaps the wind, who brings thee to me, pray?

## 30

I know not of the Heavens' turning, aught,
Nor save by spite of Fortune am I taught;
    And when I ponder on my own affairs,
A lifetime passeth and yet I know naught.

## 31

Do thou charm every heart with wooing art,
And gain at court a friend to take thy part;
    A hundred Ka'bahs equal not one heart,
Why seek the Ka'bah? rather gain a heart.

## 32

Though hue and fragrance their delights bestow,
My form as cypress, cheeks as tulips show,
    I know not wherefore my Artificer
Arrays me thus in Earth's abode of woe.

## 33

Love is chief volume of the world of thought;
The burden of youth's song with Love is fraught;
    Learn then this point that Life, in truth, is Love
Oh, thou, who of the world of Love know'st naught!

## 34

Whene'er the cup of wine in hand I drain,
And lost in drink to ecstasy attain,
    I do a hundred wonders of all sorts,
Verse flows like water from my fiery brain.

## 35

To-day is but a breath, so drink pure wine,
Once gone, thou 'lt never find this life of thine,
    Be lost in drink both day and night, since thou
Know'st well the world to ruin doth incline.

The rose said "Nothing with my face can vie."
"Yet as rose-water crushed at last am I!"
    "Count every day you laugh as 't were a year!"
The nightingale did fittingly reply.

What time of halting here falls to our share
Yields nothing save anxiety and care;
    Alas! that not one problem solved, we go
And that a thousand griefs at heart we bear!

From wine-house haunt came voice ere rise of sun,
"Ho! Tavern lounger! Mad, besotted one!
    Up! That the measure we may fill with wine,"
"Or e'er for us the measure Fate o'errun!"

### 39

Prosper, 't is not because by thee 't was planned;
Fail, it is not thy lacking, understand;
    Bow thee to Fate, submit and live content,
The world's nor good nor ill at thy command!

### 40

Be lovers aye enrapt, in fantasy,
Distraught, dishonored, touched with lunacy;
    Sober, we fret and fume o'er everything,
But drunk, say, "Let whatever will be, be!"

### 41

For God's sake in this house of vanities
With what hope sets his heart on wealth the wise?
    Whene'er he wishes to sit down to rest,
Death grasps him by the hand and bids him rise.

That fair for whom my heart hath longing vain,
Herself forlorn, some other doth enchain;
    Where shall I seek a balm to ease my pain?
Since my physician sick herself is ta'en?

### 43

The Koran though as "Word sublime" read o'er,
Men sometimes on its page, but not long, pore;
    There is a bright verse in the cup's lines, for
Within men everywhere read, evermore.

### 44

If you drink not, at sots take no offence,
Did God give grace, I would show penitence;
    "You drink not?" You commit a hundred deeds
That make my tippling boyish innocence!

### 45

O, you, come hot from that soul world below,
Amazed amid what Five, Four, Six, Sev'n show,
  Drink wine, for whence you come you do not
    know,
Rejoice! you know not whither you will go.

### 46

Where is the smoke of our fire here, O, pray?
Where profit of our stock-in-trade's array?
  To him who "Tavern-haunter" me doth call,
O, where in truth here is the tavern, say?

### 47

One wine draught to earth's kingdom doth compare
And to a thousand lives, the lid of jar!
  The cloth with which one wipes wine from the
    lips
Is worth the scarfs a thousand preachers wear!

### 48

Why grieve so much at worldly envy, pray?
Have you e'er seen the man who lives for aye?
    This one breath in your body is a loan,
With which you should live ready to repay.

### 49

So far as lies in you cause no one pain,
Lest any you inflame, your wrath restrain;
    If you desire to have eternal peace,
Though vexed, from wronging any man refrain.

### 50

O Thou, whose love and wrath made all that be,
And Heaven and Hell through all eternity,
    Thou hast Thy court in Heaven and I have naught,
Why then in Heaven is there no way for me?

### 51

I 'll drink so much wine that its sweet bouquet,
Shall when 'neath earth I go, rise from the clay
    That when some reveller passes o'er my dust,
Drunk from my wine fumes he shall reel away.

### 52

The fish to duck in droughty season said,
"What if this stream should run back in its bed?"
    "When you and I are roasted," quoth the duck,
"What matters stream, what mirage once we're dead?"

### 53

To this lost haunt with wine and love we fare,
And pledge for drink, soul, heart, cup, raiment there,
    And quit of mercy's hope and fear of law,
We 're freed from earth and water, fire and air!

### 54

Since All is unsubstantial as the air
And naught save loss and ruin; whatsoe'er
   Exists in this world, think doth not exist,
And what on earth is not, *imagine* there.

### 55

From doubt to certainty is but a breath,
A breath from unfaith's halting place to faith,
   This precious breath then do you cherish, for
Life's sum is but a breath from birth to death.

### 56

O Heaven's wheel! Ruin is thine ill behest,
Thine ancient custom ever has opprest;
   O Earth! If e'er thy bosom they should bare,
Full many a valued gem would deck thy breast!

## 57

O thou, for me of all earth set apart!
More sweet to me than eye-sight, soul and heart!
    There's naught more dear than life, O Idol! yet
A hundred times more dear to me thou art!

## 58

This two or three days' lifetime passeth on,
Like mountain stream or desert blast 't is flown;
    Still there are two days that I reckon not,
The day to come and that already gone!

## 59

That precious ruby's from another mine,
That single pearl doth bear another sign,
    The thought of this and that is vain conceit,
Love's tale hath other tongue than mine or thine.

## 60

When showers of Spring the tulips' cheeks o'erflow
Arise and to the wine-cup haste to go,
    For this green where thou sport'st to-day, per-
        chance
On some near morrow from thy dust may grow.

## 61

Now 't is young manhood's season, I design,
Since it makes glad my heart, to quaff my wine,
    Chide not the grape, though bitter yet 't is sweet,
'T is bitter since it is this life of mine.

## 62

O Heart! since 't is your fate that blood must flow,
Your state each moment change must undergo;
    What brought you, Soul, into my body, since
The end of all your strife, is forth to go!

## 63

To-day is thine, the morrow 's not for thee,
Thy care for morrows naught but grief will be;
    Nor waste this breath if thy soul 's not distraught,
For what remains of life will quickly flee.

## 64

To wine submissive we the head incline,
And pledge our souls its laughing lip to join;
    So our cup-bearer turns the flagon's throat;
So sparkles from cup's lip the soul of wine.

## 65

Knock not in vain at each door in your way,
With worldly good and ill contented stay,
    Whate'er the number on the dice of Fate
From the Sphere's cup that falls, you needs must play.

### 66

From zephyrs when my heart thy fragrance takes,
It seeks and grasps thy nature, me forsakes,
    And now there comes no thought to it of me,
For thy scent ta'en, its own thy nature makes!

### 67

The day and night were long ere thou or I,
Or on its wheeling course revolved the sky;
    Ah, softly set thy foot upon this dust,
'T was once the apple of some beauty's eye!

### 68

The idol house is as the mosque, a shrine,
And chime of striking bells service divine;
    Gueber's belt, church and rosary and cross,
Each is in truth of worshiping a sign.

## 69

Fate's marks upon the tablet still remain
As first, the Pen unmoved by bliss or bane;
    In fate whate'er must be it did ordain,
To grieve or to resist is all in vain.

## 70

Delights of both worlds revellers' bowls confine,
The sun etern in moonlit cups doth shine;
    The secret hidden in creation's soul,
If it you'd know, bides in a glass of wine.

## 71

I cannot to both good and bad unfold
My secret, nor may long tales soon be told;
    I am unable to explain my state
Or to reveal the secret that I hold.

## 72

With us base coins we no more current keep,
A broom our pleasure house of such doth sweep.
  A sage forth from the Tavern comes, and cries,
"Drink wine, since for long ages ye must sleep."

## 73

To change the written scroll there is no power,
And grieving only makes your heart bleed sore,
  Though anguish all your life consume your blood,
You cannot add to it one drop the more.

## 74

Naught save submission to God's will below,
Naught with mankind except pretense and show
  Avails.   Yea, every ruse that wit could find
I vainly tried, but Fate could ne'er o'erthrow.

## 75

My kin's my foe if he against me sin;
The stranger proving faith becomes my kin;
    If poison help me, 't is my antidote,
My poison then is baneful medicine.

## 76

No heart but bleeds at severance from Thee,
For Thee distraught are all who clearly see;
    And though Thou heed'st not any man's desire,
There's none that longeth not with Thee to be!

## 77

Seek aye the kalenders' mad tavern train,
Nor aught but wine, loved one and music's strain,
    Nor cup from hand nor jar from shoulder set;
Drink wine, O sweetheart! nor hold discourse vain!

## 78

When God of clay and water us did knead,
At Fate's blows suppliants He made us indeed;
    Still why forbid us wine? an empty hand
Is all the prohibition that we need.

## 79

Those who the head did in Death's slumber lay
Question and answer 'scape till Judgment Day.
    How long say "None bring back news from the
        dead?"
What news should they give back since naught know
        they?

## 80

From mirth while I am sober, I am freed,
When I am drunk good sense I sadly need;
    There is a state 'twixt drunk and sober quite,
I am its slave since 't is my life indeed.

### 81

The framework of the cup He did unite,
To break in rage how should God deem it right?
    So many comely heads, feet, hands and arms!
Shaped by what love, and broke in what despite?

### 82

Upon a roof I saw a man alone
Trampling some clay in scorn; in mystic tone
    The clod besought the man, "Be gentle, pray,
For thou like me wilt be much trampled on."

### 83

As tulip in the Spring her cup lifts, so
With tulip-cheeked fair, if chance serve, do you,
    And drink in gladness ere yon azure sphere
Like whirlwind suddenly doth lay you low.

## 84

I will arise intent pure wine to sip,
My cheek's hue make red as the loved one's lip;
  This busy mind—a fist well filled with wine
Into its face I'll throw to make it sleep!

## 85

Death's fear and mortal thoughts give life to thee,
And if not thence grows Life's eternal tree,
  Since Jesus breathed new life into my soul
Eternal Death hath washed his hands of me!

## 86

Since Life's affairs move not to our desire,
Of what avail our efforts, pray inquire.
  Here sit we haunted by regret for this,
We came so late, and must so soon expire.

## 87

Khayyam, O why for sin this grief and shame?
What gain in mourning thus yourself to blame?
    He knows not gracious mercy who sins not.
Why grieve?   It was for sin that mercy came.

## 88

A cloud veil shadows still the face of rose,
Desire for wine my heart and nature knows.
    Give wine O sweetheart, for the sun yet shines,
Go not to sleep, what time is 't for repose?

## 89

For none is there a way behind the veil.
Who tries to pierce its secrets but doth fail?
    The only place of rest is earth's dark breast,
Alas, that far from short should be the tale!

### 90

In this vain world, our place of brief sojourn,
Much have I searched, but this is all I learn:
    No cypress e'er can match thy form, no moon
As radiant as thy face do I discern.

### 91

In convent, school, cell, church, whate'er the creed
Are those in fear of Hell, and Heaven in need:
    But he who knows the mysteries of God,
Within his heart sows not this fruitless seed.

### 92

The world thou see'st, all's naught that thou dost see,
And everything that's said or heard by thee;
    Thou coursest Heaven from pole to pole, 't is
        naught,
Naught all thou hast in thy home's treasury!

## 93

I dreamt that Wisdom came to me and said,
" In sleep for none joy's roses petals spread,
    In life why dost thou mimic death?   Arise!
For sleep thou must when 'neath earth is thy bed."


## 94

If as it is, the heart life's secrets knew,
In death, 't would know the Heav'nly secrets too;
    But now that with yourself you nothing know,
To-morrow, from self parted, what know you?


## 95

Upon that day when sundered is the sky,
And darkened is the stars' bright galaxy,
    Upon the plain I'll seize Thy skirt and cry,
" For what sin, Idol, doom'st Thou me to die?"

## 96

Your secrets from all knaves you should conceal;
Nor should you mysteries to fools reveal;
    Your hopes you should keep close from all man-
        kind;
See you be careful how with men you deal.

## 97

Saki, since Time would shatter me and thee,
The world's no resting place for thee and me;
    Yet so the wine cup stands between us, know
We have the Truth at hand for certainty.

## 98

We 've spent life pleasure bent mid flowers and wine,
Yet Fortune ne'er supplied one need of mine;
    Though drink hath not accomplished my desire,
Ne'er doth the traveller to turn back incline.

### 99

Set wine in my hand for my heart's alight,
For swift as quicksilver this life takes flight;
    Know that youth's fire as water is, arise!
For Fortune's waking is a dream of night!

### 100

Of this wine, drink, for it is life etern;
The source of youthful pleasure, it doth burn
    Like fire, yet drink, for to the Well of Life
The briny tears of Sorrow it doth turn!

### 101

Unfit to mosque or synagogue to go,
God only of what clay I'm mixed can know;
    Like sceptic dervish or like ugly bawd,
No hope have I above, no faith below.

### 102

My wont is to drink wine, live joyously,
My creed, from doubt and dogma to be free;
    I asked the world-bride "Tell me what's thy
      dower?"
"My dowry is thy happy heart," said she.

### 103

Thy spirit to a house-dog's well compares,
'T is empty clamor that for naught else cares;
    It has the tiger's rage and wolfish craft,
'T is fox-like and it gives the sleep of hares.

### 104

Each tuft of green the river brims display,
As down on angel's lip doth grow, you'd say;
    Ah, trample not this turf! for every blade
Springs from some lovely tulip-cheeked one's clay!

One wine draught's better than the realm of Kaius
Throne of Kobad or heritage of Tus,
  More worth each sigh the lover breathes at morn
Than hypocritic zealots' shouts profuse.

Though for my sin I bad and luckless prove,
I'll not despair as heathen who do rove
  From shrine, but on the morn I die from drink
Be't Heaven or Hell I'll wish wine and my love!

A corner and two loaves our choice make we,
We've put aside earth's pomp and vanity;
  We have bought poverty with heart and soul,
In poverty great riches do we see!

## 108

If to your tress tip I do violence,
(To speak the truth and in no mystic sense.)
    Caught in your curl I see my heart distraught
To play with my own heart is no offense.

## 109

When comes the final day for me and thee
And pure from out the body then pass we,
    When we're no more, from yon blue dome full
        oft
The moon will shine on dust of thee and me!

## 110

All that's not grape juice better to eschew,
Better one old wine draught than empire new;
    Cups hundred times than realms of Feridun,
The wine-jar lid than crown of Kai Khosrau!

### 111

My drinking wine is not for pleasure's sake,
Nor sin, nor law of God or man to break,
    An instant ecstasy to gain doth cause
My revelling and me enrapt doth make.

### 112

With us the moments drag, thy lovers we,
Beside themselves, thy mourners pine for thee;
    When to our window shall thy sun return?
For more num'rous than motes thy longers be.

### 113

He's doomed to Hell, they say, who drinketh wine,
A saying 't is the heart cannot divine,
    For if all sots and lovers go to Hell,
Heaven will be empty as this palm of mine!

### 114

O Sweetheart! Heaven or Hell none e'er did see,
The man returned from that world, where is he?
    Our hopes and fears, O Heart, arise from what
Nowise save name or trace appears to be.

### 115

Wrong in Shaban, they say, 't is to drink wine,
Likewise in Rajab, 't is a month divine,
    Since Allah and His Prophet claim these months,
Through Ramazan I 'll drink, for it is mine!

### 116

From far came one with body foul to see,
The shirt he wore of Hell's smoke seemed to be;
    He broke my flask (may his life lack!), and then
"As this fine wine, so boasting man!" said he.

### 117

Many's the garb of being Heaven doth sew
Each night, and then its breast doth rend in two;
    Many's the joy and sorrow Time each day
Brings from the waters, bears to earth below.

### 118

Within the cup that flowing gem of thine,
As liquid rubies, Saki, cause to shine.
    Place, boy, within my hand, a stoup well filled,
That thus I may revive this soul of mine.

### 119

Dawn beareth night's dark curtain from the skies;
The Magian wine bring quickly, Saki, rise!
    Then up! for thy sleep will be long enough;
Yea, open those sleep-stained narcissus eyes!

### 120

The world 't is called, this ancient hostelry,
The piebald resting place of Night and Day,
 The banquet by a hundred Jamsheds left,
The tomb wherein a hundred Bahrams lay.

### 121

Now that Joy's roses fairest bloom attain,
Why from the cup your idle hand restrain?
 Drink wine, since Time is a perfidious foe,
It were hard finding such a day again.

### 122

Again the clouds come and the meads revive—
Without red wine I 'd not an instant live—
 This turf that now is my delight until
The grass from my dust joy to whom shall give?

### 123

To-day's Adina called in common phrase,
Drink wine from bowls then, in the wine-cup's place;
    And if you drink on week days but one bowl,
To-day drink two, for 't is the chief of days.

### 124

That wine that's apt in transformation,
That's plant form now and animal anon,
    Deem not its essence ever suffers change,
Itself abides, although its forms be gone.

### 125

My soul the past regretting dwells in woe;
The morrow's fears do cleave my heart in two;
    But once this my existence be set free,
Fear, anguish and regret together go.

That one on whom you do so much rely,
You'll find a foe if you ope wisdom's eye.

    It were good in this age to choose few friends,
Holding aloof from people's company.

O, fool! Naught is this image that man wears,
And naught yon vault of nine parti-hued spheres;

    Be glad that in this house of life and death
A breath we hang on, which as naught appears!

If there be minstrel, Houri, wine for thee,
And purling steam beside the flowery lea,

    Desire not better, nor fire burnt out Hell,
There is no Heaven beside, if Heaven there be.

A graybeard, drunk, forth from the inn did fare
Wine cup in hand, bearing a mat for prayer
    On shoulder. "Shaikh!" I cried, "How comes
      this state?"
"Drink wine!" quoth he, "for worldly things are air!"

When rapt, the bulbul to the garden flew,
Rose faces, smiling wine cups met his view;
    Then sang he in mine ear in ecstasy,
"Know, life once flown, can ne'er be found by you!"

Khayyam, a tent thy body typifies,
Where its Sultan, the soul, a brief time lies,
    And Death's ferrash for its next halting-place
Doth strike this tent when its Sultan doth rise.

## 132

Khayyam, who stitched tents of philosophy,
In Grief's fire fallen, was burnt suddenly,
    Death's shears cut his life's tent rope; he was sold
For nothing by the broker, Destiny.

## 133

In Spring-time if with one as Houri fair,
To verdant bank with wine-jar I repair,
    Though bad some think it, I were worse than dog
If thought of Paradise e'er enter there.

## 134

In Joy's cup sweet is wine of rosy ray,
And sweet the sound of lute and tuneful lay;
    The bigot lacking knowledge of the bowl,—
'T is sweet when he 's a thousand leagues away!

### 135

Life far from wine and saki lacketh zest,
And wanting Irac's flute notes 't is unblest;
    I find howe'er the world's state I survey
The sum of all is pleasure, naught the rest.

### 136

Since from your soul you separate, then know
Behind God's secret veil you will go, too;
    Drink wine! for you know not whence you have
        come;
Be jocund! for you know not where you go!

### 137

Since go we must, of what avail to be?
To plod the path of vain expectancy?
    Since Fate no pause for counsel gives, to rest
What boots it from that journey's thought care free?

### 138

My life-long practice is to praise the Vine
And round me have the instruments of wine;
    Zealot! if Reason guide thee here, be glad
Thy master is a pupil apt of mine!

### 139

If you will tread in Passion's steps, know you
From me that thence you will go helpless too;
    Remember who you are and whence you came,
Consider where you go and what you do.

### 140

The sky, a vault, spans our worn lives below;
Jihun a course from our strained eyes aflow;
    Hell is a spark struck by our vain distress;
Heaven but an instant when content we know.

### 141

I 'm a rebellious slave, Thy mercy show!
Make my dark soul all Thy pure light to know!
    If Heaven Thou giv'st us for obedience,
A wage 't is, where 's the bounty Thou 'd bestow?

### 142

I know not whether Allah fashioned me
For Heaven or in a horrid Hell to be;
    Cup, lute and loved one by the garden side,
All three my cash, Heaven's credit then for thee!

### 143

I quaff wine and from right and left come those
Who say, "Drink not wine which doth Faith oppose."
    By Allah! since I know Faith's foe is wine,
'T is right that I should drink the blood of foes!

## 144

The good and evil in man's mortal mould,
The joy and grief that Fate and Fortune hold,
    Impute not to the skies, for reasoned well,
More helpless they than thou a thousand fold!

## 145

Shields naught avail when by Death's arrows prest,
And honors naught, silver and gold possest;
    As far as I view worldly things, I see
Goodness alone is good and naught the rest.

## 146

The heart on little set save worldly gain,
For life to be Regret's weak mate is fain;
    Besides the mind serene and free from care,
All others only hold the seeds of pain.

### 147

No single day lost from his life hath flown,
Within whose heart the seed of cheer is sown;
    Whether he seeks obedience to God's will,
Or cup in hand in ease doth choose his own.

### 148

When God of our existence shaped the clay,
He knew our actions would be as His sway;
    Without His mandate was no sin of mine,
Then why doom me to burn on Judgment Day?

### 149

A week thou hast drunk wine continually,
Do not on Friday, then, put it from thee.
    In our creed Friday, Saturday, are one,
God worship, from day worshiping be free.

### 150

Lord, Thou art gracious, grace 't is to be kind,
The sinner forth from Iram why consigned?
    To pardon for obedience is not grace;
In pardon for rebellion grace I find.

### 151

See that the false world doth not thee ensnare,
Sit not secure!   Fate's sword is sharp, take care!
    If Fortune drop a sweetmeat in thy mouth,
Swallow it not, 't is poison mixed, beware!

### 152

Where'er there is a rose or tulip bed,
From some King's blood it takes its hue of red;
    Each violet leaf that springs from earth was once
A mole that decked the cheek of some fair maid.

### 153

Drink wine, for it is life etern, in sooth,
The fruitage of the season of thy youth;
    'T is time of roses, wine and mellow friends,
Rejoice the while, for this is life, in truth.


### 154

In our heart, Saki, is sown love of thee
Which would keep hidden to eternity.
    Spread not from pride thy skirt 'gainst worthy
        prayers
For from it our hand ne'er will loosened be.


### 155

When they say Houris' nuptials pleasant are,
"The juice of grapes is pleasant!" I aver;
    Take this cash then and let that credit go,
For pleasant is the drum beat,—heard afar!

### 156

My spirit whispered, "I crave Heavenly lore;
Instruct me then I beg if thou hast power."
 Quoth I, "Alif will do, to him who *knows*
One letter is enough, seek thou no more!"

### 157

Since coming at the first was naught of mine,
And I unwilling go by fixed design,
 Cupbearer, rise! and quickly gird thy loins!
For worldly sorrows I'll wash down in wine!

### 158

How long shall I make bricks upon the sea?
Idolater and temple weary me;
 Who says Khayyam in Hell is sure to be?
Sometimes to Hell, sometimes to Heaven goes he.

### 159

Spring's breath the rose's face doth sweetly woo,
A charmer's face makes sweet the garden too;
   To talk of yesterday were sad.   Rejoice!
To-day is sweet! of past days speak not you!

### 160

What place is this for talk?   Arise, pour wine!
To-night thy pouting lips are food for mine.
   Pour wine rose-colored as thy cheeks!   For this
My vow's disturbed as is that curl of thine.

### 161

Beyond the skies from all eternity,
My soul sought Tablet, Pen, Heaven, Hell to see;
   At length the master wisely said to me,
"Pen, Tablet, Heaven and Hell are all in thee!"

Now o'er the earth that joyousness prevails,
Each living heart the fields with yearning hails;
   On each branch is the show of Moses' hand,
And every zephyr Jesus' sigh exhales.

The Khan's crown let us sell and crest of Kai,
Turban and muslin for the pipe's soft lay;
   Then for one wine-draught let us sell at once
The chaplet, courier of deceit's array.

Out on that heart wherein love hath no sway
Nor love-mad to the witching one a prey;
   The day that thou dost pass devoid of love,
For thee is none more wasted than that day.

### 165

Rejoice with wine for 't is as Mahmud's reign,
List to the lute that sounds as David's strain;
    Be glad to-day, for 't is to be desired,
Of past or future think thou not again.

### 166

Ten Powers and Nine Spheres, Eight Heavens
    enrolled,
And Planets Seven of Six Sides He enscrolled;
    From Senses Five, Four Elements, Three Souls,
    God
In Two Worlds, man! like thee but ONE did mould!

### 167

Though silver store the wise doth not avail,
And moneyless, earth's garden 's but a jail,
    With purse of gold the haughty rose doth smile,
While empty-handed droops the violet frail.

### 168

As I the potters' quarter pass some day,
I 'll think myself a pot 'mid pots' array;
    They yet may make a wine-jar I may drain
Before to potters I present my clay.

### 169

Before the grave doth take its fill of me,
Or e'er all my parts prostrate scattered be,
    O, wine, from flagon's tomb uplift thy head,
My dead soul may become alive to thee!

### 170

Stern Fate hath blood of many a mortal shed,
And leaves of many a new-blown rose wide spread;
    Of youth and beauty be not proud, O boy!
For many a bud 's strewn o'er the garden bed!

### 171

Save Truth, no law is fit to rule the wise
No life is fit that His command defies;
    Whatever is, is as it had to be,
And naught exists that should be otherwise.

### 172

This golden bowl, and vault of azure hue,
Full oft have rolled and will the ages through;
    And likewise, we, impelled by turns of Fate,
Like others come, and go like others, too.

### 173

Since God did set in order Nature's frame,
Why should He cast it down in scorn and shame?
    If good, how comes it He doth break His work?
And if not good, why are these shapes to blame?

## 174

Kindness to friend and foe, 't is well to show,
Then how will he whose nature 's good, ill do?
    The friend whom you ill-treat your foe becomes,
But kindness changes to a friend, your foe.

## 175

To Wisdom's eye what matters foul or fair,
Or if the lovelorn silk or sackcloth wear?
    What brick or pillow under lovers' heads?
To Heaven or Hell bound what do lovers care?

## 176

Drink wine, for e'en in winter you may see
The world's wits' wine sweat down their necks roll free.
    How say "Broken's your vow"? A hundred vows
Than one wine flask far better broken be!

### 177

The flowers blossom, Vintner, wine bring me!
Your hand withhold from acts of piety;
    These few days ere Doom trap us, we'll enjoy
The red wine and the loved one's company.

### 178

We've traversed many a vale and desert plain,
And did all quarters of the world attain;
    But heard of none who came this road, the way
The traveller goes, he comes not back again.

### 179

The Tavern prospers from our drinking wine,
Blood of remorse be on thy head and mine,
    If I ne'er sinned, what then would Mercy do?
For Mercy but awaits my sin and thine.

Lo, from the world what vantage have I gained?
    Naught.
What profit of my life in hand retained?   Naught.
   I'm Jamshed's bowl, but what when 't is crushed?
    Naught.
Joy's torch am I, what when its light has waned?
    Naught.

When at life's brink, what's Balkh, what's Nishapur?
What sweet or bitter when the cup brims o'er?
   Drink wine for many a moon will wax and wane
Through changing months when we are here no more.

A cup of rubies pure give, Saki, pray!
That my heart's fire its liquid may allay,
   While Reason, boy, shall grasp my spirit's rein,
Still on the skirt of wine my hand shall stay!

## 183

Devotion profits not the devotee,
For practice, Saki, proves it certainly;
    The flowing beaker fill, boy, quickly, for
Whatever is, is from eternity.

## 184

He who earth, sky and heaven did array,
Full many a scar on grieving hearts doth lay,
    And many a ruby lip and musky tress
Hath buried in earth's treasure chest of clay.

## 185

Oh, fools, the world's allurements do not buy
Since ye know her conditions certainly;
    Your precious lifetime give not to the winds,
Haste to drink wine and to the loved one fly!

## 186

O, my companions, nourish me with wine!
This amber-hued face make like rubies shine;
    When I am dead, wash me with wine, and shape
My coffin planks from timber of the vine!

## 187

The Day They girthed the coursers of the sky,
The Pleiads decked and Jupiter on high,
    This lot of ours was writ in Fate's divan,
Why blame us since Heaven wrought our destiny?

## 188

Alas! the "raw" oft well cooked viands eat,
The "incomplete" have worldly gear complete,
    And that mere boys and lackeys should possess
The smiles of charming Turkish beauties sweet!

## 189

He first in weakness me to being brought,
And save amaze to life hath added aught;
    Unwilling we depart, and whence is this
Our coming, being, going, we know naught.

## 190

When o'er my mind doth pass my sins' disgrace,
From my breast's fire, tears trickle down my face,
    Yet meet 't is always when a slave repents
The master should grant pardon of his grace.

## 191

What time before the pride of life had flown,
It seemed to me few secrets were unknown;
    Since modest grown, I see in reason's way,
My life is spent and naught is surely known.

### 192

They who 've become the flower of all mankind,
Drive to the zenith the Borác of Mind,
    Yet in Thy essence' knowledge like Heaven's
        wheel
Themselves, heads dazed, o'erturned and whirling,
        find!

### 193

Now that of pleasures only names remain,
No old friend left, and but new wine to drain,
    To-day when, save the cup, naught is at hand,
Then from the flask do not Joy's hand restrain.

### 194

O, long the world will last when gone are we,
Without a name or trace of thee or me;
    Before, we were not,—and there was no void,—
And after, when we 're not, the same 't will be.

### 195

Those who have worn the earth beneath their tread,
Who seeking Him o'er both the worlds have sped,
    I never have been told that they this case
Have as it is, aright interpreted.

### 196

Since God in Paradise hath promised wine,
Why in both worlds is 't banned by law divine?
    Some Arab hamstrung Hamzah's camel once,
For this our Prophet drinking did enjoin.

### 197

In rose-time, king, how should a man like me
Forbear from minstrel, wine and company?
    The garden, wine-jar, lute-player better are
Than Houris, Heaven and Kausar's stream will be.

## 198

If thy cheek idol be, idolatry
And thy cup's drinking is more sweet to me,
  Love-drunken for that reason I've become,
Since than a thousand lives 't will sweeter be.


## 199

Alas! that riches from our hands have fled,
And blood of many a heart Death's hand hath shed.
  And from that world comes none that I may ask
"How fare the travelers who have thither sped?"


## 200

Strange all these nobles who high honors have,
In pain and grief of their lives quittance crave,
  And yet they hardly reckon as a man
Him who unlike them is not Passion's slave.

Oppressive from the first this wheel on high
Will ne'er for any one his knot untie,
    Where'er a wounded heart it doth espy,
To add another wound it straight doth try.

Would'st Life's foundations find secure to be?
And in this world awhile the heart care free?
    From drinking wine sit not apart, and so
Life's pleasures ever find vouchsafed to thee.

With rose-hued wine in this abode below,
O wise man, mix your earthy substance so
    That each mote of your dust They give the wind,
May wine-soaked to the tavern threshold go!

### 204

Whene'er the violet her robe's color shows,
And zephyr spreads the garment of the rose,
　　He's wise who drinks with silver-bosomed maids
And on the stones the empty wine-cup throws.

### 205

To kiss thy foot, O lamp of my delight!
Than other's lip kisses is better quite!
　　My hand thy fancy's hem doth clasp all day,
And my foot springs to meet thee every night!

### 206

No room for joyance have hearts filled with woe,
Thy loss makes hearts else glad, with grief to flow;
　　With thee, I this world's bitter have made sweet,
With thy loss' bitterness what shall I do?

### 207

Since never may we grasp truth's certainty,
One must all his life long a doubter be.
    Let me beware lest I set cup from hand;
Where's drunk or sober when in ecstasy?

### 208

My food for soul and body wine will be,
The solver of each hidden mystery;
    Naught else I seek in this world or the next,
One single draught contains both worlds for me.

### 209

Closed is the volume of my youthful day,
And this fresh Spring-time gladness gone for aye;
    Yon bird of joy named Youth, ah!  I knew not
When here you came nor when you flew away!

### 210

With these few feeble folk the world who own,
Who witless, knowledge think is theirs alone,
    Be calm, since those not asses such as they,
By them are damned as skeptics every one.

### 211

With revellers joyous be the hostelry,
And burnt the pious skirt of devotee;
    That hundred-patch coat and blue woolen robe
'Neath feet of dreg-drainers still fallen be!

### 212

How long the slave of scent and hue remain?
How long all ill or good seek to attain?
    Though Zamzam's fount or from Life's well-
        spring, thou
Within earth's breast at last wilt sink again.

### 213

Till cheering wine the Friend before me place,
No kiss Heaven prints on either foot or face;
    They say "Repent in time!" but how repent
Till Allah of His goodness giveth grace?

### 214

When I am dead my clay do ye make fine,
That my state be to men a warning sign;
    With grape juice wet my body's dust, and shape
Therefrom a cover for a jar of wine.

### 215

Khayyam, though of the blue that spans us o'er
The tent be pitched and closed Discussion's door,
    The Everlasting Saki in Life's bowl
Thousands of bubbles like Khayyam doth pour.

### 216

Since Time will have no bounds, be of good cheer,
The stars will spangle still the Heavenly Sphere;
    With bricks that from your body they will mould
Walls of another's dwelling, men will rear.

### 217

In wine ablution must in taverns be,
For none a sullied name from blot can free;
    Its liquor pour, for none can now repair,
So torn it is, our veil of modesty.

### 218

In hope a lifetime to the winds I gave,
Nor one glad day of that time did I have;
    From which I fear lest Fate give not enough
Of time to take the justice that I crave.

### 219

In life's affairs one should on guard remain,
And speech concerning worldly things restrain,
    Be as one lacking tongue and eye and ear,
While ear and tongue and eye you still retain.

### 220

Whoso is now of half a loaf possest,
Himself to shelter hath a little nest,
    Who slaves for none nor is by any served,
Let him be glad for he hath this world's best.

### 221

Naught adds my service to Thy majesty,
And my past sin abateth naught from Thee;
    Then pardon and retract not since I know
Thou 'rt slow to blame and swift in clemency.

The juice of grapes may my hand ever bear
And my heart ever long for Houri fair:
    They say "God give thee penitence!" He 'll not.
Far be 't from me! Repentance I forswear!

Alas! that book and pulpit hands like mine
Should touch, that hold the flask and cup of wine!
    Zealot! thou 'rt dry and I a lover moist,
I ne'er heard wet would catch that fire of thine!

None in this world attains a rose-cheeked fair
Till in his heart Fate driven the thorn he wear;
    See, in this comb until a hundred teeth
Were cut, it ne'er might touch the loved one's hair!

### 225

When we depart the world is not distressed;
Nor one pierced of a hundred pearls possessed;
    Alas! a hundred thousand subtle thoughts
From people's ignorance die unexpressed!

### 226

Nor hot nor cold, the air breathes sweet to-day,
And clouds have washed the rose cheeks' dust away;
    And ever to pale rose the nightingale
"Thou must drink wine!" in ecstasy doth say.

### 227

Ere you the blows of darkling Fate sustain
Bid them to bring you rose-hued wine to drain;
You are not gold, O heedless dolt, that men
Hide you in earth and then dig up again!

My coming brought no profit to the sky,
My going adds not to its majesty
    Or pomp, from none have my two ears e'er heard,
Coming or going, the true reason why.

To heavy hearts is wine both plume and wing,
Wine, beauty's mark to wisdom's cheek doth bring;
    All Ramazan no drop we've drunk; 't is past
The Festal night comes, Shawwal ushering.

No night but all bewildered is my soul,
And down my breast tears big as pearls do roll;
    My head from grieving is not filled with wine,
For none when 't is upset can fill the bowl.

Why will you life in self-adorement spend,
Or "Is" and "Is not" strive to comprehend?
    Drink! since Death presses at Life's heels, 't is
       best
In dreams or drink it pass on to the end.

Deluded, some fall in their vanity,
Some seeking Houris that are said to be,
    But when the veil Fate lifts, it will be seen
How far they 've fall'n from thy way, far from Thee.

In Heaven, they say, dwell dark-eyed Houris fair,
And that pure wine and honey will be there;
    If wine and woman we love here, 't is right
Since all the same 's the end of the affair.

My soul in this net drawn, time and again
Shamed of her earth-mate, to be free is fain;
    Methought to break this jail, did not my foot
Law's stirrup holding, from the stones restrain.

Wine pour, to dance a mountain 't would incline;
Lacking indeed is he who lacketh wine;
    It is a soul to animate this frame;
How would you bid me then the cup decline?

They 've seen the moon of Ramazan, they say;
Then for a month from drink I 'll turn away;
    At next Sha'ban's end so much wine I 'll pour
That drunk they 'll find me till the Festal day!

### 237

Life's vintage, now mere dregs, now clear doth run;
We sackcloth wear, and silken garb anon;
 All this is of small moment to the sage,
Of slight account since Death is coming on.

### 238

None the eternal secrets e'er can trace,
Nor one step, foot beyond his nature place;
 From pupil to the master I behold
Those born of woman, weak in every case.

### 239

The world crave less and live contentedly,
Of earthly good and evil cut the tie;
 Be light of heart as are these circling skies,
A little while they stay, and then pass by.

### 240

There will be at the Rising, they pretend,
A parleying, and hasty our dear Friend;
    From perfect goodness naught save good can come,
Be light of heart, 't will be well in the end.

### 241

A thousand devotees one cup of wine
Is worth and one wine-draught the realm of Chin,
    Its bitter is a thousand sweet lives worth,
What sweeter on the face of earth hath been?

### 242

O, Soul, seek not the frail ones' company,
And cease with love affairs engrossed to be.
    Frequent the doorways of the Dervishes,
Then the Elect may make a choice of thee.

From thought of wealth or want the heart to free,
And two and seventy Creeds' perplexity,
    Drink wine, for take one draught, a thousand ills
It cures, forswear not then its alchemy.

To drink wine though forbidden, yet this ban
Is as to measure, company and man;
    These three conditions being right, then say,
If wine a wise man cannot drink, who can?

A one-maund cup of wine I 'll brimming make,
Yea, of two cups of rich wine I 'll partake;
    First, Faith and Reason I will thrice divorce,
Then the Grape's daughter for my bride I 'll take.

### 246

Cupbearer, since to Life there is no guide,
Better than wine and cup there's naught beside.
    Of old, it is our friend, for no such fire
Doth in Life's stream or Kausar's fount abide.

### 247

The sigh that to no friend escapes from me,
The word that to no mate could spoken be,
    If I found any heard excepting Thee,
In truth, I should expire instantly.

### 248

Than Jamshed's bowl thy cheek, boy, is more fair;
Than Life Etern thy way's Death better were;
    To every dust mote of thy foot that lights
My face, ten myriad suns could not compare!

### 249

Boy, of that wine that is my faith and soul,
A cup! for 't is of my sweet life the whole;
    If it is not your wont to quaff its juice,
'T is mine with sweetheart fair to drain the bowl.

### 250

What time the rising dawn's blue light doth shine,
Your hand should grasp the goblet of pure wine;
    They say the truth tastes bitter in the mouth,
It must be "Truth" is wine then, by this sign.

### 251

'T is time when earth its tender verdure wears,
And Musa-like froth on the bough appears,
    The clouds open their eyes in vernal showers,
And Jesus' breathing ones the earth uprears.

### 252

Thy body burden not with toil and pain
White silver store or yellow gold to gain;
    The foe will feast on thee, then feast with friends
Or ever thy warm breath wax cold again.

### 253

Each draught the cupbearer pours on the clay
Its fire of grief in some eye doth allay;
    Praise Allah that you see wine is a juice
That takes your hundred pangs of heart away.

### 254

Friends, when in concord ye meet and whene'er
The cupbearer the Magian wine doth bear,
    Delighting in each other's charms, O, see
A helpless one ye think on in your prayer!

### 255

Not once has Heaven been kind in my affairs,
Nor in my favor with sweet voice declares,
    No day breathe I in joy that I'm not given
Into the clutches of a hundred Cares.

### 256

If in two days a loaf of bread one gain,
And water from a broken jar can drain,
    Why take commands of one less than yourself?
Or why to serve one like yourself remain?

### 257

While Moon and Venus circle in the sky,
Better than ruby wine I naught espy;
    I wonder at the wine-sellers, for they,
Better than that they sell what will they buy?

## 258

Those strong in virtue and of learning deep,
Whose merits joined lights for their fellows keep
    Have found no way out of this darksome night,
They 've told their tale, and then gone back to sleep.

## 259

The heavens above from clouds shower eglantine,
You 'd say that blossoms rained upon the green,
    In lily cups I 'll turn rose-colored wine,
Since, violet-hued, the clouds pour jessamine.

## 260

My aged head by love of thee is caught,
Else why my hand and cup together brought?
    My sweetheart broke the vows of reason born,
And Time hath torn the garment Patience wrought.

### 261

I 'm not the man whom death doth fill with fear,
That half than this to me hath more of cheer;
    To me life is a loan that God hath made,
And I 'll repay it when the time is here.

### 262

The stars that are the dwellers of these skies,
Occasion much conjecture to the wise,
    See you lose not the end of Wisdom's thread,
For those who rule are dizzied with surmise.

### 263

The stars that Heaven for a while adorn,
That come and go and back with earth are borne,
    Now on Heaven's skirt, now in the pouch of earth,
While God dies not shall aye anew be born.

### 264

Those who are slaves of wit and subtle thought,
Fretting o'er " Is " and " Is not " come to naught.
    Go, with the wise drink grape-juice, for these
        fools
From unripe grapes to raisins have been brought.

### 265

The sense which bids you Pleasure's path pursue,
Whispers a hundred times a day to you,
    " This moment have in mind, for you 're no plant
Which when they mow it down, springs up anew ! "

### 266

Now Ramazan is past, Shawwal is here,
The time of greeting, feasting, song is near;
    'T is time when skins on shoulders they cry out,
" Behold the porters one by one appear ! "

### 267

All our dear friends have from our handclasp gone,
Beneath the foot of Death fall'n one by one;
  They drank with us two or three rounds before
At Life's feast and enrapt lie overthrown.

### 268

When in the mould my clay They mixed of old,
With it They mingled evils manifold;
  Better than this I am I cannot be,
For as I am They poured me in the mould.

### 269

Those joyous ones who of old wine drink deep,
And they who in the prayer-niche vigil keep,
  Not one is on dry land, but all at sea,
ONE only wakes, the others are asleep!

## 270

My seed They 've with Non-being's water sown,
And from the fire of grief my soul has grown,
    And like the wind about the world I 'm blown,
Till They at last my scattered dust have strewn.

## 271

Since in this age from wisdom is no gain
And save the thoughtless none Life's wine-cup drain,
    Bring forth that juice which reason doth efface,
So Fortune us to favor will be fain.

## 272

When the Soul's mistress doth depart this home,
Back to its origin each part doth come;
    This lute of Life's four silken strings then from
The stroke of Fortune's bow untuned become.

### 273

Of yon Sphere telling varied tales they keep,
These fools who thread the pearl of science deep,
    Since ne'er expert in Heaven's mysteries,
They wag the chin and then return to sleep.

### 274

These folks are sorry asses all the same,
Skins full of emptiness like drums, a name
    Acquire, if you would have them kiss your foot,
For they are all the very slaves of fame.

### 275

On that Day when reward in each degree
Will be, They as thy wisdom will rate thee;
    For goodness strive, for on the Judgment Day
Thy rising will be as thy quality.

### 276

The Bowl-maker who our head-bowls hath made,
Thus doing His own qualities portrayed;
    One He inverted o'er our being's board
And to that head-bowl passion He did add.

### 277

My attitude toward Thee I would make plain,
And that I will abridge in verses twain:
    "For love of Thee in dust I'll lay my head,
That with Thy love I may arise again."

### 278

The heart a lamp is, lit at beauty's cheek,
And though by grief consumed new life doth seek,
    Like flame with moth the heart is, one should say,
For thus the saw, "With burning, fire doth take."

## 279

Companions, when ye meet as ye agree,
Your friend ye needs must pledge in memory;
    And when together wholesome wine ye drink,
And my time comes, turn down a glass for me.

## 280

At first such grace and favor why did'st show?
Delights and blandishments on me bestow?
    And now thou strivest to afflict my heart;
What wrong I may have done I fain would know.

## 281

Those hither come that in ambition vie,
Distraught by drink, pleasures and luxury,
    The goblet drain and silent in the earth
Wrapt in the sleep of Naught together lie.

### 282

Of Fortune's bounty thy full portion seize,
Take cup in hand, on Joy's couch sit at ease;
    God recks not of obedience or sin,
Take of the world thy fill, as thou dost please.

### 283

Since Heaven increases nothing but our pain,
And gives naught that it takes not back again,
    The unborn ne'er would hither come if they
But knew what we at Fortune's hands sustain.

### 284

Why of existence have a care, O, friend?
With idle thought thy heart and soul to rend?
    Live blithely, let the world glide merrily,
They ne'er consulted thee about the end.

### 285

Yon dwellers in the tombs are dust and clay,
Escaped from self, of all things witless they;
    Their every atom scattered, wide, alas!
What a mirage they make till Judgment Day!

### 286

O, Heart, suppose all worldly goods thy dower,
Adorned with verdure be thy pleasure's bower,
    Then on that verdure like the dew at night
Resting, and vanished in the morning hour!

### 287

Heed not Traditions nor the Law Divine,
Withhold from none the morsel that is thine,
    None slander, nor afflict thou any heart,
I warrant thee the world beyond,—bring wine!

## 288

Through Fortune's shifts that for the vile doth care,
A hundred griefs and pains through life I bear,
  Like heart-closed bud within life's rosary,
Like time-scarred tulip that doth blood spots wear.

## 289

Youth is the better time in which to taste
Pure wine by comely striplings' presence graced;
  As this vain world was ruined by a flood,
'T is best in it be drunk, by wine laid waste.

## 290

The world's astir and mad in quest of Thee,
Bare before Thee stand wealth and poverty;
  To all Thou speakest but each ear is deaf,
With all art present but no eye can see.

### 291

With churl ill-bred and stupid best beware
You drink not, for he 'll bring a deal of care;
    The night of joy, noise, drinking, brawl, next day
His headaches and excuses you will bear.

### 292

Since there 's no 'scaping what the stars decree,
Fret not so much in seeking—vanity;
    Nor on thy heart so great a burden place,
To leave it and pass on the end will be.

### 293

Drink pure wine, Soul, when roses scent the air,
Toasting the graceful, heart-alluring fair;
    "Wine is the Grape's blood, and 't is lawful made;
Drink my sweet vintage!" doth the Grape declare.

### 294

Are you depressed?   Then take of *bang* a grain,
And next a pint of rose-hued grape-juice drain.
  "Sufi you are?   Nor eat of this nor that?"
Go!   Feast on stones, since stones your fare remain!

### 295

In the Bazaar I saw but yesterday
A potter pounding hard a lump of clay;
  The clay cried out to him in mystic tones,
"I once was like thee, treat me gently, pray!"

### 296

One wine-draught's better than the realm of Jam,
The cup's perfume than food of Miriam.
  Ah!   Sweeter toper's sighs at break of dawn
Than songs of Bu Sa'id and Bin Adham!

### 297

Hid in the circle of the Heavenly vast,
A cup that all must drink in turn is placed;
   Sigh not when thy time comes, but gladly drink,
For then it is thy turn the cup to taste!

### 298

Though thy years two, three, or ten hundred be,
From this old house They'll helpless carry thee;
   Then be thou king or beggar of bazaar,
These both at the same price the end will see.

### 299

Abandon wife and child if Him you'd find,
From self cut bravely bonds to self that bind;
   The things of earth but clog you on your way,
How fare with them? Free them and leave behind!

### 300

O, Heart! Since earth's truth is illusion vain,
Why so distressed in lasting grief and pain?
    Bear trouble! Bow to Fate! Once gone the Pen
For thee will never trace the scroll again!

### 301

Where's one returned of all who went before,
To us the long road's secret to tell o'er?
    Take care in this house ('t is but metaphor),
That naught you leave for you'll return no more.

### 302

This Sphere that makes to none its secrets plain,
Hath thousands like Mahmud and Ayaz slain;
    Drink! For the Fates to no one twice give life,
For none who leaves the world returns again.

### 303

Thou, who surpasseth all earth's kings in might!
Know'st thou when wine can make the spirit bright?
    On Sunday, Monday, Tuesday, Wednesday and
On Thursday, Friday, Saturday, morn and night.

### 304

O, ogling, sweet, inconstant and fair maid!
Be still! a thousand troubles are allayed;
    Thou bid'st me look not on thee.  This command
Is as if "Hold awry, spill not!" were said.

### 305

In taverns better I commune with Thee
Than far from Thee in mosques feign piety;
    O Thou of all created first and last!
If Thou wilt, burn, if Thou wilt, cherish me!

### 306

When wine thou drink'st, wit's outcast do not be,
Thy mind the dwelling of insanity.
  Would'st have its ruddy juice allowed to thee?
Restrain thy wrath, seek no man's injury!

### 307

With fair maid and red wine by marge of rill,
Of joy and mirth the while I take my fill;
  I was not but I am, and yet will be,
I have drunk and drink now and will drink still.

### 308

Seek thou with wise and worthy men to be;
A thousand leagues from worthless people flee;
  Drink poison that the wise give but refuse
The antidote a fool doth offer thee.

## 309

A bird flown from the mystic world am I,
That from below to heights above might fly,
    Since here I find no worthy confidant,
I go by the same door I entered by.

## 310

That abstinence from her could never be,
God ordered and then bade me from her flee;
    'Twixt these commands we mortals stand per-
        plexed,
As bidden "Hold awry, spill not!" were we.

## 311

They're gone and none returns to tell to thee
Of those passed on the Veil's deep mystery;
    Thy needs, not texts but true prayer will reveal,
Mere play is prayer without sincerity.

### 312

Go! On earth's face, in Heaven's face high in air
Fling dust, drink wine and woo the sweet-faced fair!
    What time is there for worship? What for prayer?
For none of all those gone returneth e'er.

### 313

If I Thy service' pearl did never thread,
Nor sin's dust ever wiped from off my head,
    For all this of Thy mercy I have hope,
Because that "One is two" I ne'er have said.

### 314

Whenever Grief thy heart's attendant be
With self-affairs in deep perplexity,
    The case thou should'st seek of some other heart,
So full contentment shall result to thee.

### 315

Our drinking habit we 've begun anew,
And to the "Five Prayers" have we said adieu;
   Where'er the goblet is, our necks stretched out
Just like the necks of bottles you may view.

### 316

Joy seek not, for Life's sum is but a sigh;
Each mote is from dust of a Jam or Kai.
   The world's case and the root of this life is
A dream, vain phantasm in a breath passed by.

### 317

In truth and not by way of simile,
Heaven plays the game and its mere puppets we;
   In sport moved on Life's chess-board, one by one
We reach the chess-box of Nonentity!

### 318

What is this fleeting life dost ask of me?
Were I to tell, its story long would be.
   'T is but a breath, felt, wafted from some sea,
And then blown back to depths of that same sea!

### 319

My loved one (be her life long as my pain!)
To-day began to favor me again,
   She glanced at my sad eyes and passed as if
To say "Do good! and cast it on the main!"

### 320

I prest my lip in yearning to the urn,
Thereby the means of length of life to learn,
   And lip to my lip placed it whispered low,
"Drink!  For to this world you will ne'er return!"

### 321

The thorn that bends 'neath every creature's tread,
May spring from some love's curl, fair brow of maid,
 And every tile on palace battlement
Some Vizier's finger be or Sultan's head!

### 322

Thou say'st "Rise! hold!" as in Naught's lair I lay,
"Bide in the world, from its strife far away!"
 Now I'm bewildered quite by Thy command,
As if Thou "Hold awry, spill not!" did'st say.

### 323

O, Thou, who all men's secret thoughts dost know,
In case of need who succor dost bestow,
 O, Lord give me repentance and forgive,
Thou from whom penitence and pardon flow!

### 324

I saw a bird perched on the wall of Tus,
Before her lay the skull of King Kaius,
    And thus she moaned, "Alas! Where sound thy
      bells?
Where the alarums of thy drums profuse?"

### 325

Seek not the forecast of Futurity,
Nor ask of aught that comes since it must flee.
    This ready-money moment count as gain,
Reck not of Past, nor ask of times to be.

### 326

To start yon golden bowl its course who made,
Earth's solid base, how end thus firmly laid,
    By Learning's touchstone ne'er will be assayed
Nor ever in Conjecture's scales be weighed!

### 327

My ignorance I expose how frequently!
My heart is saddened in perplexity.
    Do you know why I wear the Magian belt?
'T is of my Moslemism ashamed am I.

### 328

Khayyam, rejoice if overcome with wine
Thou with a tulip-cheeked one dost recline;
    Since all things end in naught, rejoice and think
How 't would be wert thou dead, whilst life is thine.

### 329

Last night I went into a pottery,
Two thousand pots did silent, speaking see.
    "The potter, buyer, seller, where are they?"
One of the vessels cried out suddenly.

### 330

Wine, that blest Khizer guards securely,
Life's water is and its Elias I.
    The food of heart and soul I call it, for
God says, "A boon 't is to humanity."

### 331

Though 't is forbidden, yet drink wine for aye,
With lute and minstrelsy both night and day;
    And of its ruby liquor spill a drop,
And drain all that remains then, if you may.

### 332

By mead and stream when roses scent the air,
Be with thy friends and mate as Houri fair;
    Bring forth the cup! For those who drink at
        dawn
Give mosque nor synagogue nor thought nor care.

### 333

Would'st thou attain the stage of mystery?
See that to none thou doest injury;
 Brood not o'er death nor fret for daily bread,
For both in their own time will come to thee.


### 334

My virtues singly note, by the half score
My faults forgive, past sins O God, pass o'er!
 O, let not whiff and gust Thy wrath's flame fan!
By Allah's Prophet's dust I grace implore!


### 335

How long let future ill your heart depress?
Far-seeing people's portion is distress;
 Be blithe! Let not the world weigh down your
  heart!
To fret will make your lot, nor more nor less.

### 336

There is a cup Creative Wisdom makes,
That from Love's care a hundred graces takes;
 Yet this frail urn the Potter of the world
So shapes,—then on the ground in pieces breaks!

### 337

Wine in the crystal is a subtle sprite,
And in the flask it is a fluid bright.
 No heavy-wits are fit to be my friends
Save wine-flasks, which are heavy and yet light.

### 338

Thou, knowing not of bread or salt the tie
Still flay'st me like a fish, O wheel on high!
 By woman's wheel since all mankind is clothed,
'T is better far than thou, wheel of the sky!

### 339

If roses be not ours, behold the thorn!
And darkness, if comes not the light of morn!
    And if we lack the vestment, cell and shaikh,
Behold bell, church, and girdle to adorn!

### 340

Thou of the final fire art not afraid,
Nor cleansing in Contrition's stream hast made;
    I fear when Death's blast puts out thy life-lamp,
That Earth will spurn thee in her bosom laid!

### 341

Lo! Dawn appears! and rends Night's robe in twain:
Why grieve? Arise! the draught of morning drain!
    O, Sweetheart, drink! for many a breaking Dawn
Will look for us when we are dust again!

## 342

How long will prate of all eternity?
'T is past my science and my theory;
    Wine has no substitute in time of joy,
'T is wine for every riddle turns the key.

## 343

Of God your Maker, merciful in sway,
Despair not for your sins, though great be they;
    For though to-day you die in a debauch,
He will absolve your crumbling bones, next day.

## 344

Thy course contents me not, O, wheel on high,
Free me, unsuited to thy destiny;
    If thou dost favor fools and witless ones,
I too am such, nor worth nor wit have I.

### 345

This form of life is pictured phantasy,
Who knows this not, unknowing quite is he:
   Sit, drain the wine-cup and be gay and free
From these the figments of vain imagery!

### 346

Love in perfection and charmer fair!
Heart full of speech though tongue be speaking ne'er!
   What is more strange on earth O Lord, than this?
I thirst; a limpid stream flows by me there!

### 347

At all times drain the brimming cup and free
Your mind from grieving vain; delighted be
   With the Grape's daughter sitting, though forbid
Far better than her lawful mother she.

### 348

Some wine! and be its trickling murmur made
To bulbul's song, nightingale's serenade!
    Wine ne'er would gurgle from the flagon's throat,
If right were drinking without music's aid!


### 349

Questioning will not solve Truth's mystery,
No, nor will money spent nor property;
    Till rent thy soul, thou drink'st blood fifty years
The way from "words" to "states" They'll not
      show thee.


### 350

Up from Earth's center e'en to Saturn's throne,
I solved all problems of the Heavenly zone;
    From bonds of fraud and artifice leaped out,
And every barrier burst save Death's alone.

### 351

'T is well with cup to fill the heart with glee,
And count as little "has been" and "to be."
    This borrowed soul a pris'ner here below,
A while from Reason's bondage we'll set free.

### 352

The moment when at Death's behest I flee,
And like a leaf I fall from Being's tree,
    The world in my heart's joy I'll sift away
Ere dustmen in their sieves to dust turn me.

### 353

This wheel of Heaven which we amazed discern,
Is like a Chinese lantern, as we learn;
    The Sun the lamp, the World the lantern is,
And we like figures are that on it turn.

## 354

O, Lord! It was Thou who my clay did'st knead.
    What should I do?
And of my silk and wool did'st spin the thread.
    What should I do?
  All good and bad that from my being come,
It was Thou who did'st write upon my head. What
    should I do?

## 355

Friend, let us not the Morrow's fears forecast,
Come! profit by this moment while it last;
  To-morrow this old Inn we'll quit and be
The comrades of Seven Thousand Ages past!

## 356

No moment while you may refuse wine's aid,
For by it reason, heart and faith are stayed;
  Had Iblis drunk one drop, to Adam he
Two thousand salutations would have made.

### 357

The door of Hope I 've shut to self, that so
Favors I may escape from high and low;
    I 've but one Friend who takes my hand, I know
That which I am, I am, and He doth know!

### 358

A measure dance! while we clap hands, arise!
Wine flown, we drink to thy Narcissus eyes.
    In twenty cups is not so much delight,
But in three score amazing pleasure lies!

### 359

By circling Heaven I 'm saddened constantly,
And with my own base nature vexed am I;
    Wit lacking from the world to sit apart,
And wanting wisdom free from earth to fly.

Upon earth's carpet sleepers I espy,
And others hidden underneath descry,
    And those gone or not come I see where'er
I view the desert of Nonentity.

Of sin I reck not, since I trust Thy grace,
Nor with Thy care, the toilsome way I trace,
    And I rate not the "black book" at a grain,
So that Thy favor shall make white my face.

Think not a fear to leave the world have I,
Nor dying nor that thence the soul should fly;
    Since death is certain, that I do not dread,
'T is my ill living makes me fear to die.

### 363

How long mere slaves of petty prudence be?
What if we live a day or century?
    Wine bring us in the bowl, or ever we
Become but wine-jars in the pottery.

### 364

You and I to twin compasses compare,
O soul! one body though two heads we bear;
    We circle now around a central point
Till we at last again united are.

### 365

How long, O stupid zealot, wilt thou chide,
That ever wine-flown we in taverns bide?
    Thou sadly wear'st thy beads, pretence, deceit;
With sweetheart, song and wine we're satisfied!